KT-528-169

bodymatters

kate smokes
cigarettes

Janine amos

CHERRYTREE BOOKS

bodymatters
Kate Smokes Cigarettes
Jon Drinks Alcohol
Why Won't Kim Eat?
Is Helen Pregnant?
Alex Does Drugs
Jamal is Overweight

A Cherrytree Book

First published 2002
by Cherrytree Press
327 High Street
Slough
Berkshire
SL1 1TX

© Evans Brothers Limited 2002

British Library Cataloguing in Publication Data

Amos, Janine
Kate smokes cigarettes. - (Bodymatters)
1. Smoking - Juvenile literature 2. Tobacco
habit - Juvenile literature 3. Tobacco -
Physiological effect - Juvenile literature
I. Title
362.2'96

ISBN 1842341081

Printed in Hong Kong by Wing King Tong Co Ltd

Acknowledgements
Planning and production: Discovery Books
Editor: Patience Coster
Photographer: David Simson
Designer: Keith Williams
Artwork: Fred van Deelen
Consultant: Dr Gillian Rice

**All the characters appearing in this book
are played by models.**

Picture acknowledgements
The publisher would like to thank
the following for permission to
reproduce their pictures: Corbis 28
(Steve Chenn); Chris Fairclough 5;
Photofusion 26 (Clarissa Leahy);
Science Photo Library 14.

kate smokes cigarettes

contents

Kate's new friend, Maria, is having a party.

Kate has been looking forward to it for days. Kate's boyfriend, Suhas, has been invited too. When Kate and Suhas reach Maria's house, an older girl answers the door.

'Hi, come in. I'm Beth, Maria's big sister,' she says.

Kate and Suhas find Maria in the living room with Megan and Alice from school.

'You didn't tell me you had a big sister,' Kate says to Maria. 'She's really cool!'

It's a hot day, so they all go out into the garden. Kate sees that Beth has come too. The older girl is holding a packet of cigarettes.

'Who wants one?' asks Beth, offering the packet round.

Megan says she does.

'Smoking's bad for you,' says Suhas, going back to the house. 'It gives you cancer.'

'Scaredy cat!' laughs Beth, as she

a cigarette?

Cigarettes are made from the dried leaves of the tobacco plant, which is grown in many warm parts of the world. Cigarette smoke contains thousands of chemicals. Many of them are dangerous to our bodies. Forty-three of them are known to cause cancer.

The chemicals in cigarette smoke include acetone (also found in nail varnish remover), hydrogen cyanide (a poison), formaldehyde (also used to preserve dead bodies) and ammonia (also found in dry-cleaning fluids). The smoke contains poisonous gases – carbon monoxide and nitrogen oxide – and tar, a brown sticky liquid which can damage people's lungs. Cigarette smoke contains a drug called nicotine, too.

5

lights Megan's cigarette.

the first effe

Kate's worried. She's promised her parents that she'll never smoke. But she doesn't want to be the odd one out.

'You're such a baby, Kate!' laughs Beth.

'All right,' says Kate at last. She puts the cigarette in her mouth. 'They can't be that bad. My mum smokes all the time and she's OK.'

Beth lights the cigarette and Kate copies the others. The first puff chokes her and she doesn't like the taste. She splutters out the smoke. Her head starts to spin and she feels sick. **'Keep going. Yo**

6

# of nicotine

Nicotine is poisonous if taken in large amounts.

Smokers take in only small amounts of nicotine at a time.

As Kate smokes the cigarette, the nicotine goes straight to her lungs. It then passes into her bloodstream. Seconds later, it reaches her brain. When this happens, the nicotine makes Kate's head spin and the spinning makes her feel sick.

It takes just fifteen seconds for nicotine to reach the smoker's brain.

7

:o it,' Beth tells her.

nicotine

By the end of the afternoon Kate has smoked three cigarettes.

She is used to the taste. Now she likes how smoking makes her feel.

'Smoking's cool!' Kate giggles, as she and Suhas make their way home in the dark. 'I feel really grown up.'

'You look really stupid!' Suhas tells her. 'And you smell awful. You'd better not let your mum and dad find out what you've been up to!'

The nicotine works in Kate's brain to give her feelings of pleasure

In the body

9

Once the nicotine reaches Kate's brain, it works on the part that controls feelings of pleasure. It causes a sudden rush of good feelings – but they don't last. Most of the effects of the nicotine will disappear from Kate's body after about thirty minutes, leaving her feeling low. Kate will need another cigarette to get those good feelings back again.

At the same time, the nicotine puts a strain on Kate's heart, making it beat faster. It also raises her blood pressure. Kate's heart has to work harder to pump the blood around her body.

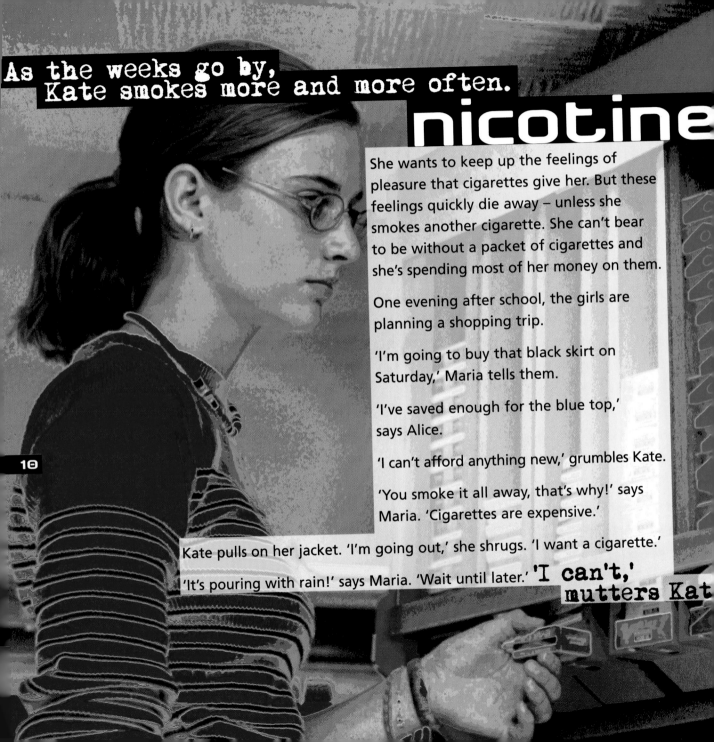

As the weeks go by, Kate smokes more and more often.

nicotine

She wants to keep up the feelings of pleasure that cigarettes give her. But these feelings quickly die away – unless she smokes another cigarette. She can't bear to be without a packet of cigarettes and she's spending most of her money on them.

One evening after school, the girls are planning a shopping trip.

'I'm going to buy that black skirt on Saturday,' Maria tells them.

'I've saved enough for the blue top,' says Alice.

'I can't afford anything new,' grumbles Kate.

'You smoke it all away, that's why!' says Maria. 'Cigarettes are expensive.'

Kate pulls on her jacket. 'I'm going out,' she shrugs. 'I want a cigarette.'

'It's pouring with rain!' says Maria. 'Wait until later.' 'I can't,' mutters Kate

10

addiction

11·00   13·50   15·30   17·45

Kate is smoking so much because she has become addicted to nicotine. This means that her body is unable to do without it. Nicotine is a powerfully addictive drug. Kate needs to keep up a certain level of nicotine in her body throughout the day to feel 'normal'. If she doesn't smoke, she gets a strong need, or craving, for a cigarette. She feels miserable and snappy.

11

I need one now.'

Running makes her cough. Her chest hurts.

'You can't run like you used to,' Suhas tells her. 'It's all that smoking. You'll make yourself ill.'

chemicals

'Leave me alone!' snaps Kate. 'It's *my* body!'

Suhas walks home with Kate. When they get there, Kate's mum and dad are waiting for her. They look worried.

'We've had some bad news,' Kate's mum, Lorna, tells her. 'Grandad has got cancer in his throat.'

'Is it because he smokes so many cigarettes?' asks Kate in a small voice.

'Yes,' says Dad. 'He's smoked two packets a day ever since I can remember. I think he started when he was about your age, Kate.'

'Will Grandad die?' Kate asks.

'The doctors think he'll be OK,' Lorna says. 'But he'l for an operation.'

12

n the body

Some of the harmful effects of smoking may show up quite quickly. Kate's cough is caused by the smoke irritating her lungs. When they are irritated, the lungs produce a slimy substance, called mucus, as a protection. This extra mucus makes Kate cough. Smoking also sends carbon monoxide into her bloodstream. This means that less oxygen is carried around her body, so Kate feels breathless.

Kate's clothes and hair smell of stale tobacco and she has bad breath.

13

.ave to go to hospital

When Kate's family go to visit Grandad in hospital, Lorna tells Kate about Grandad's operation.

'The surgeon has cut a hole in his throat where the cancer was,' she explains gently. 'Later, they'll fix a metal piece there to help Grandad speak. But at the moment he won't be able to talk to us.'

At the hospital, Grandad is lying in bed. There's a white bandage at the front of his neck. Kate can't stop staring at it. Kate tells Grandad all about the goal Suhas scored in football. Grandad can't answer her so he writes 'Well done!' on a notepad. Before they leave Kate gives Grandad a big hug.

Back home, Kate gets the box of old photographs down from the cupboard. She hunts through them until she finds one of Grandad as a young boy. Kate is feeling scared.

'I'm going to try to stop smoking right now,' sh

14

of the throat

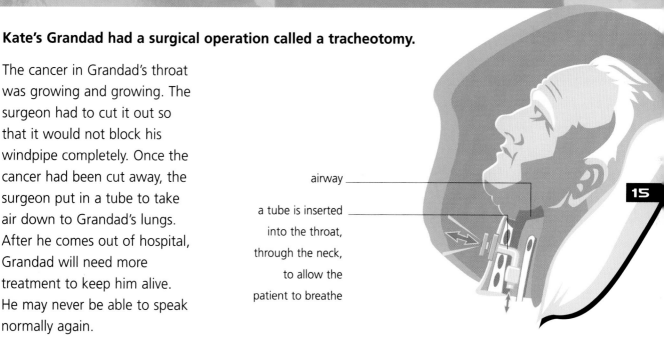

Kate's Grandad had a surgical operation called a tracheotomy.

The cancer in Grandad's throat was growing and growing. The surgeon had to cut it out so that it would not block his windpipe completely. Once the cancer had been cut away, the surgeon put in a tube to take air down to Grandad's lungs. After he comes out of hospital, Grandad will need more treatment to keep him alive. He may never be able to speak normally again.

airway

a tube is inserted into the throat, through the neck, to allow the patient to breathe

15

romises herself. **'I don't want to end up like Grandad.'**

withdrawal

Her body wants a cigarette badly. She feels tired and cross and she can't relax.

Kate keeps going to the fridge for snacks. She has a lunch date with Suhas. But when he arrives at her house, Suhas finds Kate searching in the fridge for a yogurt.

'You won't want any lunch at this rate!' he remarks.

'Mind your own business!' shouts Kate. 'I don't feel like eating out, I've got a headache. I'm going round to Alice's.'

Kate arrives at Alice's house in tears.

'I've stopped smoking but I feel terrible,' she wails. 'I keep arguing with everyone. I'm dizzy and tired and hungry all the time. I can't stop thinking about cigarettes, I want one so much!'

16

'Well done for stopping!' says Alice. 'Come on, let's go for a walk to take your mind off smoking.'

They take some snacks with them.

'Here, have an apple and some carrots. Every time you want to smoke, eat something healthy instead!' suggests Alice. 'That'

symptoms

Kate's body is missing the nicotine it is used to. The unpleasant feelings she has now are called withdrawal symptoms. They will be strongest for the next forty-eight hours and they will continue off and on for several weeks.

Kate feels dizzy because her body is now getting extra oxygen. Her craving for nicotine makes her think she's hungry. She also wants to keep putting something into her mouth. She is tired because her body misses the buzz that nicotine gave her. She has headaches much of the time.

Kate is doing lots of good things to help with her withdrawal symptoms. She is talking about her problem. She is having some exercise to take her mind off cigarettes. She is eating healthy snacks. Most importantly, she is not giving in to her strong desire for just one more cigarette.

17

ow my mum stopped last year.'

At the weekend, Kate and Alice go into town. Beth and her friends are on the corner, smoking.

'Have a ciggie, Kate,' offers Beth.

'No thanks,' says Kate. 'I don't smoke any more.'

'Boring!' sneers Beth.

'It's cool,' says Kate, tossing her head. 'I've saved loads of money already.'

18

'Were you tempted?' asks Alice as they walk away. 'Of course I was,' Kate tells her.

'But I know that if I have one, I'll start all over again. Anyway, I'm saving up for

selling cigarettes

Few people begin to smoke as adults. Most smokers take up the habit when they are teenagers. The law is strict about the age at which young people may buy cigarettes. But many shopkeepers break the law and sell to people who are underage.

In western countries, the law is strict about cigarette advertising too. Advertisements are no longer allowed to show smokers as healthy, glamorous, wealthy or successful. But cigarette companies find other ways to advertise their products – for example, through powerful photographic posters or free gifts. Some cigarette companies sponsor sports events. The names of their cigarettes appear on television when the event is shown.

Governments throughout the world make huge amounts of money from the sale of cigarettes by charging tax on them. Every time someone buys a packet of cigarettes, some of the money goes to the government. This adds up to millions of pounds every year.

some new clothes now!'

19

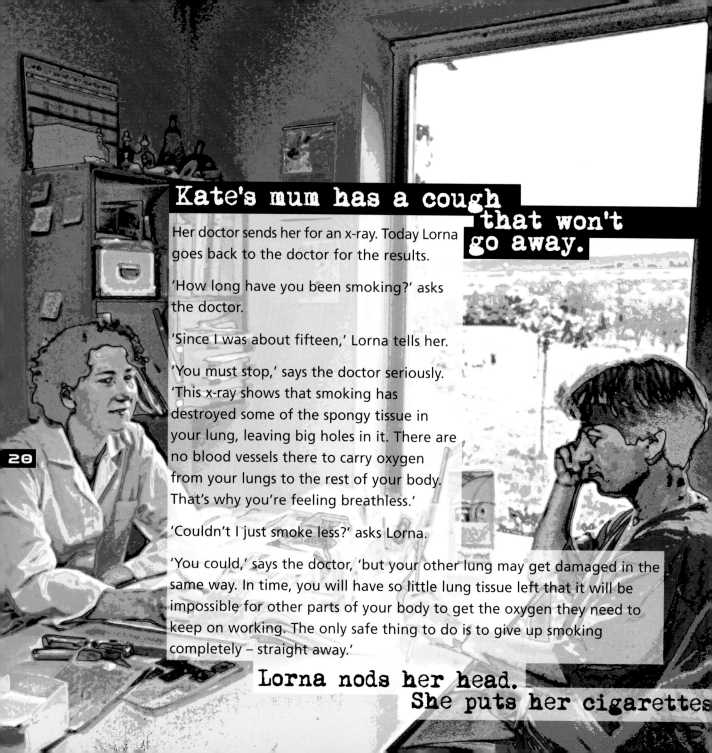

Kate's mum has a cough that won't go away.

Her doctor sends her for an x-ray. Today Lorna goes back to the doctor for the results.

'How long have you been smoking?' asks the doctor.

'Since I was about fifteen,' Lorna tells her.

'You must stop,' says the doctor seriously. 'This x-ray shows that smoking has destroyed some of the spongy tissue in your lung, leaving big holes in it. There are no blood vessels there to carry oxygen from your lungs to the rest of your body. That's why you're feeling breathless.'

'Couldn't I just smoke less?' asks Lorna.

'You could,' says the doctor, 'but your other lung may get damaged in the same way. In time, you will have so little lung tissue left that it will be impossible for other parts of your body to get the oxygen they need to keep on working. The only safe thing to do is to give up smoking completely – straight away.'

Lorna nods her head.
She puts her cigarettes

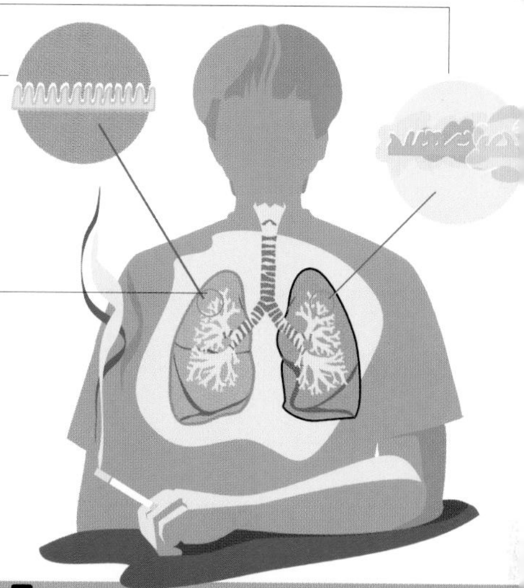
cilia damaged by smoking
healthy cilia
mucus and tar build up in the lungs, causing the smoker to cough

smoking and the lungs

Your lungs are two large spongy organs that fill most of your chest. They contain millions of tiny tubes and air sacs. In these air sacs oxygen is passed into the blood.

The air passages are lined with hairs called cilia. The cilia act like tiny brushes, sweeping away germs and dirt from the lungs. Regular smoking has caused Lorna's lungs to be full of extra mucus and tar. The cilia are damaged and can't do their work. Bacteria get trapped in the sticky mucus and cause infection. Lorna's lungs try to protect themselves by producing more mucus. Lorna coughs and coughs.

Over time, smoking has damaged the spongy tissue of Lorna's lungs. They are now like worn elastic, stretched out of shape. This makes it hard for her to breathe and not enough oxygen gets into her bloodstream. Lorna feels breathless nearly all the time.

in the doctor's waste-bin.

Lorna has been smoking for twenty-five years. Smoking is part of her life.

Lorna needs some help to give up smoking. Here are some things she might try:

Nicotine patches

Adults can buy these at chemists. They look like big plasters which smokers place on their arms. Patches provide nicotine without the other harmful chemicals contained in cigarettes. They give the person who wears them a dose of nicotine through the skin. The dose is lowered as the weeks go by. This reduces the withdrawal symptoms

She tries to watch television but she can't relax. She goes to bed early but can't sleep. Her body needs a cigarette.

Lorna manages not to smoke for two days. She finds it hardest at work. She's used to having a cigarette while she sorts out problems on the telephone. She's used to smoking with her coffee and at lunchtime. Lorna's headache comes back. She can't concentrate. At last she asks a friend for a cigarette.

'I'll just have one,' she thinks.

As well as facing the physical withdrawal symptoms of giving up nicotine, she will have to cope with stopping the habit of her adult lifetime. She is used to the feel of a cigarette between her fingers and in her mouth.

As soon as Lorna gets home from the doctor's she wants a cigarette. She feels angry and frustrated. She has a headache. Lorna shouts at Kate and grumbles at her husband. She walks up and down the room.

By the evening a packet of cigarettes and

caused by stopping. Smokers can learn to give up the habit without fighting the withdrawal symptoms at the same time.

Nicotine gum

Like nicotine patches, this chewing gum provides adults with a dose of nicotine without the other chemicals. Nicotine passes into the body through the sides of the mouth.

Hypnosis

Some people believe that hypnosis helps them to give up smoking. The hypnotist puts the smoker into a relaxed, trance-like state, which makes his or her mind more open to suggestion. In this state the smoker can be encouraged to give up the habit.

Acupuncture

If someone wants to stop smoking, acupuncture may help. The acupuncturist inserts needles under the skin at particular points on the body. This treatment may help with other addictions too.

help for giving up

hypnosis   acupuncture   patches   gum

Support

Smokers can ask their friends not to offer them cigarettes. They can ask their families to understand if they become snappy while they give up. They can ask for their help to take their minds off cigarettes by going with them for walks, cycle rides, or to the gym. Their families can help them by saying, 'Well done'.

Lorna has bought herself
she's smoked
        them all.

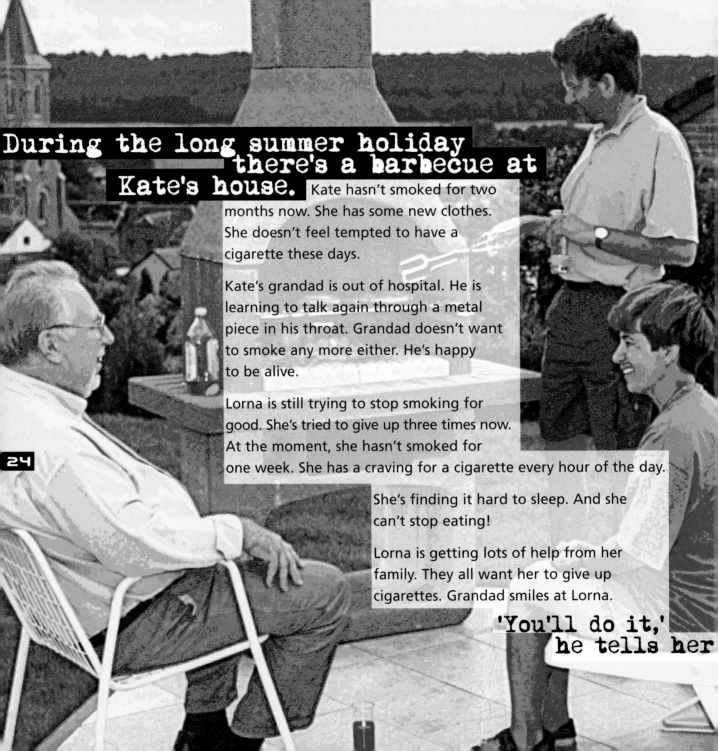

During the long summer holiday there's a barbecue at Kate's house.

Kate hasn't smoked for two months now. She has some new clothes. She doesn't feel tempted to have a cigarette these days.

Kate's grandad is out of hospital. He is learning to talk again through a metal piece in his throat. Grandad doesn't want to smoke any more either. He's happy to be alive.

Lorna is still trying to stop smoking for good. She's tried to give up three times now. At the moment, she hasn't smoked for one week. She has a craving for a cigarette every hour of the day.

She's finding it hard to sleep. And she can't stop eating!

Lorna is getting lots of help from her family. They all want her to give up cigarettes. Grandad smiles at Lorna.

'You'll do it,' he tells her

giving up for good

Smoking and lung cancer

Smoking is the cause of eight out of every ten deaths from lung cancer. The younger a person is when they start smoking, the greater their risk of getting this disease. Cancer-forming chemicals in cigarette smoke travel to the air tubes in the lungs. These chemicals attack normal cells and may cause them to become cancerous. They multiply and crowd out the normal cells. The cancer cells form a lump called a tumour, which can spread to other parts of the body. When smokers give up, their risk of getting lung cancer starts to decrease.

'If I can give up, anyone can.'

trachea (windpipe)

healthy lung

bronchus (tube leading from trachea to lung)

diseased lung with tumour

25

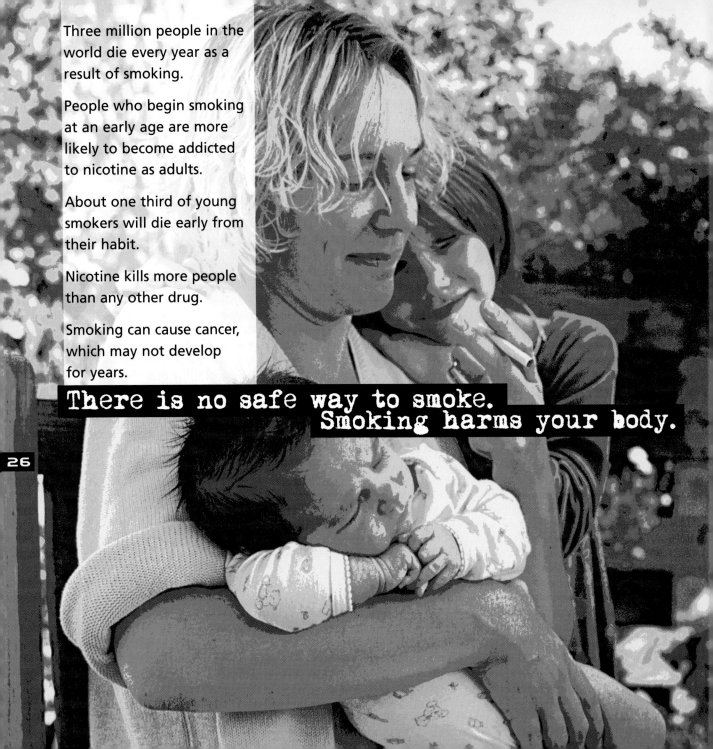

Three million people in the world die every year as a result of smoking.

People who begin smoking at an early age are more likely to become addicted to nicotine as adults.

About one third of young smokers will die early from their habit.

Nicotine kills more people than any other drug.

Smoking can cause cancer, which may not develop for years.

There is no safe way to smoke.
Smoking harms your body.

smoking facts

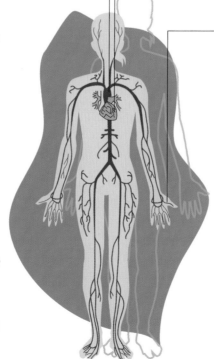

heart

aorta (main artery)

the system of arteries throughout the body

Secondhand smoke

Have you ever been in a room where lots of people were smoking? If so, did your eyes water? Did you want to cough? Breathing in other people's cigarette smoke is called passive smoking. It can cause lung cancer in non-smokers. It may also increase their risk of heart disease.

Children whose parents smoke are more likely to have chest infections and breathing problems. Passive smoking can make asthma and hay fever worse. It makes non-smokers' skin, hair and clothes smell too.

Smoking and heart disease

The heart is a powerful muscle and needs a good supply of oxygen to work properly. Oxygen travels to the heart in tubes called arteries.

As people grow older, their arteries may become clogged up and the flow of blood to the heart is reduced. Chemicals in tobacco smoke speed up this process.

Smokers are more likely than non-smokers to die young from heart disease.

Some good reasons for giving up smoking
(or never starting)

People who don't smoke live longer than those who do.

Smoking causes early wrinkles, bad breath, bad-smelling hair and clothes, and yellow nails.

Smoking increases your risk of getting lung cancer, heart attacks and many other diseases.

Smoking can reduce your chance of success in sports by causing chest illnesses and coughs.

Smoking is expensive. Multiply the cost of your daily cigarettes by 365 days a year. Now multiply that by five. Think of all the money you will burn away in five years. Think what you could spend it on if you saved it!

Smoking harms the health of people around you.

Most offices, public building.

It can be hard to say no when everyone else is smoking. Practise saying no with a friend at home – or on your own in front of a mirror. Remember – cigarettes can kill you. They make your breath, hair and clothes smell and stain your teeth. They are also expensive. Say, 'No, thanks,' clearly and firmly.

'No, thanks, I don't smoke.'
'No, thanks, I don't like the taste.'
'No, thanks, smoking's a drag!'

Make friends with non-smokers. Passive smoking harms your health. It's safer to be around people who don't smoke.

saying no
to cigarettes

Remember – smoking doesn't:

Make you look more grown up

Help you to stay slim

Help you to get an older boyfriend or girlfriend

Make you popular

29

public transport, concert venues and sporting events are fast becoming smoke-free. Finding somewhere to smoke is a hassle.

glossary

addicted being so dependent on a drug that you are unwell if you don't take it. Drugs that cause your body to become dependent on them are called addictive drugs.

asthma a breathing disorder, often accompanied by a tight feeling in the chest.

bacteria tiny living things which live in some parts of the body. Many bacteria are helpful but some are harmful, causing disease and infection. We call harmful bacteria 'germs'.

blood vessels the tubes that carry blood around the body.

cilia tiny hairs which line the air passages in the lungs. They move together in waves, trapping dirt and germs and pushing them out of the lungs.

craving a powerful longing for a drug.

drug a chemical that changes the way the body and mind work.

hay fever a reaction to pollen, dust etc. The sufferer sneezes a lot and has a runny nose and watery eyes.

nicotine a poisonous chemical found in the roots, leaves and seeds of the tobacco plant. Nicotine is an addictive drug.

organ a part of the body with a particular job to do. Your heart, lungs, eyes and brain are all organs. An organ is made up of different kinds of body tissue joined together.

tissue the material of which the body is made.

withdrawal symptoms the unpleasant or painful effects of giving up an addictive drug. The withdrawal symptoms of nicotine can include headaches, feeling sick and dizzy, tired, cross and worried, being unable to sleep and having difficulty concentrating.

further information

Getting Help

If you have a problem with smoking there are people who can help. Talk to an adult you trust. Go to your doctor. You could also phone one of the organizations listed below. Sometimes the telephone lines are busy. If they are, don't give up – keep trying.

Quitline Freephone 0800 002200

ChildLine Freephone 0800 1111

Websites The following websites have information about giving up smoking:
http://www.tacade.com
http://www.quit.org.uk

index